Evil Revelations

Thoughts of Good vs. Evil

Dianna Collier

BookLeaf Publishing

India | USA | UK

Made with ❤ on the BookLeaf Publishing Platform
www.bookleafpub.in
www.bookleafpub.com

Dedication

This book is dedicated to my parents David and Patricia Bassett who taught me good values, charity and the love of God. I also dedicate this to all those I love that have already passed through Heaven's gate. Amen

Preface

"Evil Revelations" delves into the eternal struggle between light and darkness, good and evil, within and around us. Through vivid imagery and haunting narratives, these verses explore themes of temptation, sin, faith, and redemption, offering a mirror to the battles we all face.

This collection invites you to reflect on the choices that define us and the forces that shape our souls. Step into this world of shadows and light and discover the revelations that await.

Acknowledgements

Thank you to the community at St. John The Evangelist Church in Streamwood, who have taught me so much about the church, catholic faith and the Trinity (*God, Jesus and the Holy Spirit*).

1. Cathedral of Evil

Where is my church
The devil said
I wanted it painted
Blood red

There will be a crown
Everyone must wear a frown
On their knees they must be
When they worship me

Diamonds and gems must be given
There is no forgiveness
Destruction is his business
Satan is his religion

No songs will be sung
No bells will be rung
All are meet with sadness and grief
Don't expect to be released

His speech is blasphemy
Amazed at his audacity
Sharing his fantasy
With profanity and insanity

The congregation are fools
Faithful though treated cruel
His ways are unjust
Full of lust and mistrust

The soul must give submission
Carry out his mission
Never to be free
You are his for eternity

2. Dancing Demons

Demons dancing all around
Laughing at tortured sounds
Deep in the ground
Music playing loud

Through the mirror a reflection
Celebrating Armageddon
To the devil you are presented
Another demon is invented

From the depths below
The devil wields his mighty sword
Wanting to slay our Lord
Knock down Heaven's door

Naked women chained to the throne
Their fate already known
Demons watch as they moan
Praising him with screams and groans

Look the devil in the eye
With agony you will die
To Hell you have descended
By the devil you are selected

3. Deal for my Soul

Belief in my soul is misplaced
My head a black lonely space
Need for my pain to be gone
Never felt so alone

No happiness within my life
Looking for respite
All I have is grief and sorrow
How do I make it through tomorrow

Suddenly the devil appears
Wanting to make a deal
Offering me an appeal
He could take away my tears

Turn back the mistakes of my years
Remove all my fears
Allow me to feel joy again
All my problems he could mend

All I need to do is give him my soul
Don't worry you can keep it until you are old
Think of all the happy times
All you have to do is sign

Sorry, this I cannot do
As Jesus came before you
It is to him my soul belongs
It is for Jesus I long

He will give to me all that you offer
Now is my time to suffer
Don't you see he is carrying me
Until it is time to set me free

4. Devil's Lair

The Devil is in his hole
Listening to Rock n Roll
Puffy on a bowl
Feeding his black soul

Living in a lavish house
Spread out on his couch
Wishing he was not alone
No one to love heart of stone

Angry he is stuck here
Surrounded by fear
Cannot shed a tear
Only the evil leer

Wild women appear
Giving him a beer
The party will begin
For a night of lust and sin

Starts fires in a flash
The air smells like ash
Wishing for a cool breeze
Where he can relax at ease

He should never had angered God
Sent to Hell with a nod
Time for him to learn his place
Lucky he is not lost in space

5. Evil Thoughts

The devil is in my ear
Causing me to shiver in fear
Listening to the things he says
Brings me nothing but dread

He tries to tell me God is dead
To get inside my head
Trying to take me from God's bread
Evil thoughts he sends

He plays on my anger
Trying to make me madder
Vengeance I should take
Make them pay for their mistake

Lust is what he makes me feel
My thoughts of others seem real
Sweat runs down my flesh
The devil gives me no rest

Feeling the greed
Money is what I need
On others misery I feed
As he plants his evil seed

In prayer I must plead
To help me stop the bleed
God is all I need
To have my mind freed

6. Faithless

Sympathy for the faithless
Who will remain nameless
Their actions are shameful
The results are painful

Today the youth
Searching for the truth
Focused on their goals
Their future in their control

All they need is money
To make their day sunny
Reaching for gold
Forgetting about their soul

A life of greed
Doing anything to succeed
Of power they feed
Fulfilling their need

Cheating on their misses
Stealing other's kisses
Thinking Jesus is a superstition
Worshiping their riches

Everlasting life is a fairy tale
Alone when they fail
Don't know how to pray
To help them through their day

Walking alone through good and bad
When you are happy or sad
No one to offer strength
When your will breaks

In God they do not believe
Do not desire to be freed
They give God no petitions
As they go about their ambitions

7. Gluttony

You are a coward
No willpower
Paying the toll
For no self-control

Stuffing your face like a pig
Overlooking your butt is big
No willpower when offered sweets
Living for that sweet release

Taking it all for yourself
Not caring about anyone else
Your deals are full of malice and greed
Taking from those who need

Your actions are extreme
Filled with immoralities
Relying on debaucheries
Within your depravities

Gluttony is the term
A lesson you must learn
A deadly sin a darkened phase
That leads to ruin all your days

8. Hellelujah vs. Hallelujah

Hellelujah a party is roaring
Cocaine on the mirrors
Joints being rolled
People drunk falling to their knees

Clubs and bars
Liquor and gambling
Bar tabs and tips
Fights and gossip

Blasphemy and abuse
Using others to satisfy their lust
Hiding their addiction
Ashamed of what they have become

Worried about their destiny
Hiding from their past
Ignoring their family
Pushing God from their hearts

Hallelujah a choir is singing
Bibles on the tables
Hosts in the chalice
People kneeling to God in the pews

Churches, Chapels
Holy Land, Temples
Donations, Preaching
Charity, Community

Praising the Lord for his sacrifice
Worshiping his deeds
Crucifixes, Crosses
Displayed with pride

Accepting their destiny
Embracing the past and future
Showing love to family and friends
Holding God close to their heart

So what do you say Hellelujah or Hallelujah
Do you hold God in your heart
Will you spend your eternity in heaven or hell
Is your soul for sale or will you hear the church bell

9. Highway to Hell

What happens when the Devil drives the bus
Allowing for greed, addiction, and lust
Beautiful women showing their busts
Leaving the Lord in the dust

It is an unending party
Passing around the bacardi
The devil is building his army
Tempting his victims with a ferrari

Giving away drugs for free
Your destruction he will foresee
He will not hear your plea
Focused on you being his devotee

Playing on your fantasies
Forgetting what you believe
Driving you to insanity
Going against humanity

Yelling with profanity
At your friends and family
Life turning to a calamity
All part of his strategy

Thinking you have confidentiality
Allowing the brutality
Buying into his flattery
Ignoring reality

He takes your vitality
Losing your chance at immortality
Confused on your sexuality
Changing your life substantially

You don't see the gravity
Taking your morality
It is a tragedy
Joining him in anarchy

10. Hunter of the Night

Devil Hunter wild and brave
Tracking demons through the cave
Traveling through the dark of night
Listening for any sound or show of might

Looking for the Devil's Lair
Feels the fear but does not care
His soul is filled with light
As God will help him through the fight

Armed with water, pure and bright
Silver bullets for the fight
Wooden spite, a heavy club
Ready for battle no foe to love

Unsure of what will draw blood
Crucifix gleams in the moonlit flood
Guns on his hip, his grips stays tight
Belt of clips for the coming fight

Not sure what he will encounter
Not sure what defense has been mounted
Need to catch the devil alone
Away from his mighty throne

Experienced at hunting evil
Every kill gives him a thrill
It is not a sin to kill the devil
Watching for the situation to unravel

Not all evil shows it's face at night
Not all give him a fight
What he is doing he knows is just
For in his heart in God he trusts

11. Lust

Lust must be controlled
It will take its toll
Doing what is unjust
To satisfy your lust

Leaving your wife in the dust
Losing all her trust
Everything goes bust
All because of your lust

Craving love and compassion
Yearning for passion
Giving into your obsession
Leading to depression

A price will be paid for your debauchery
It will affect your morality
Realizing your treachery
Making the family feel awfully

A high price to pay for your sexual desires
Adultery forgiveness is required
Lust causes many trails
For forgiveness pray to the Messiah

12. Original Sin

Born with sin
Within us when life begins
We will struggle to win
Fighting with a grin

The evil is in our skin
Always at the fringe
We need baptism to rinse
Taking the Lord as our prince

Why do I do what I don't want to do
Why do I get into these moods
Commit to unwanted feuds
Not following the rules

It is by choice
To select God and rejoice
Hearing his voice, so bold and grand
Stopping the devil with his command

For sin can spoil
Cause many foils
From sin we should swiftly recoil
To ease our hearts and end the toil

Upon his cross
We place our loss
Life of divinity and infinity
Belief in the trinity

Sin cannot win
With belief our life begins
It all starts from within
Feeling God within our skin

13. Pride

Pride is of value after a great achievement
Experienced when you sense fulfillment
Shown in response to praise in gratification
Displaying team satisfaction

Pride can quickly turn to overconfidence
Walking around with self-importance
Showing off your arrogance
Treating others with haughtiness

Proud men usually look down on others
Not caring of the opinions of another
It is through pride that the devil
Became a sinful rebel

Shows no pleasure in having something
Only that the other man has nothing
Everything he owns must be the best
Showing off to all the rest

Power and money become your only loyalty
Concerned about yourself and not unity
Showing off your superiority
Your dealings have no dignity

Exhibiting self-admiration
Feeding your self-esteem
Inflating your self-worth
Flaunting self-importance

The devil is leading you towards doom
Your downfall will come soon
Showing God no honor
Not worshipping the Father

Shadows grow where pride takes hold
A heart grows lifeless, dark, and cold
Pride is a spiritual cancer
It is not the answer

14. Sex, Drugs, and Rock & Roll

Sex, Drugs and Rock & Roll
Will it cost your soul
Does it praise the occult
Causes youth to get lost

Will it cause afflictions
Feed your addictions
Needing something for the head
While listening to the Grateful Dead

Led Zeppelin speaks of the Stairway to Heaven
Where AC\DC prefers the Highway to Hell
Leading youth to abuse
Promoting alcohol and drug use

Hoping the buzz will last
Think I need another blast
Partying with all my friends
Hoping the night will never end

Dating within your group
Pregnancy in your youth
Your dreams are now dead
You are now lost in your head

Passing a joint
Making a point
Sharing an idea
Making a deal

Alcohol leads to bad decisions
Causes many divisions
Rock & Roll moves my soul
Listen until I am old

15. Son of the Devil

The Devil's son grew his wings
Dark as night, when spread the demons sing
Eyes of fire, grin as bright as pearls
Tall and slender, his temper burns

Taking over the earth
Drowning out God's mirth
Looking for a way to break his bounds
Wearing his devilish crown

His ways are money, lust and greed
Tempting all who share his beliefs
Looking for the souls of the damned
Doing all that he commands

No soul to rely
No conscience all lies
He wants to go to Heaven's gate
To destroy those of faith

The righteous fight for salvation
God's army protects heaven's foundation
The armies will clash
Angels and demons will crash

A battle of all times
Bright light of God will blind
Swords will be their weapon
Angels will prevent Armageddon

The devil will fall again
Back to Hell in torment
Jesus our souls he did defend
On him we can all depend

16. Soul to Steal

Some people have no tomorrow
Only a tale of sorrow
Sitting alone in their tower
Devil with too much power

The devil went out
Looking for a soul to steal
Finding someone in despair
Willing to make a deal

What can he offer this lost soul
To mark his soul as sold
Money, fame or health
A good life full of wealth

It is a roll of the dice
Selection must be right
Make sure no angels are in sight
To help them in their fight

To take away their eternal life
No more watching for the light
Looking for someone who is greedy
Someone who is needy

Someone who cares not
Someone with a lonely heart
Someone in grief
Someone with no belief

Lucky in this world they are easy to find
Worry and fear crowding their mind
Sign the contract
You will be mine

17. Tales of Dread

One day the devil slyly said
How to get into the children's head
Through fairy tales with fear they're fed
Filling their dreams with endless dread

Humpty Dumpty falls, he's dead
Jack and Jill break heads instead
The cradle drops, the baby cries
The witch burns Hansel as he fries

Three blind mice lose tails with a knife
A spider scares Miss Muffet for life
The Pied Piper takes children away
The Emperor struts in disarray

Parents read with gentle intent
Unaware of the malice meant
Rocking their kids to sleep with care
While nightmares linger in the air

Teach them of Jesus, strong and kind
With love and hope to fill their mind
Start with His word to guide their way
Show them joy with each new day

Let them dream of light and peace
Of love that makes their fears decrease
Give them hope to help them soar
Tales of dread will haunt no more

18. The Pit

Dark and gloomy
No more beauty
Unhappiness and cruelty
The devil's grip consumes me

Souls are lost in the deep
Nothing to do but weep
Never to sleep
Punishment will be steep

The future is bleak
Anxiety will peak
No longer can speak
Escape they seek

Feeling weak
Smell of fear will reek
Struck there for keeps
Listening to the shrieks

Heaven you cannot reach
Boundary cannot be breached
Many souls trapped in a ditch
Stuck between took the Devil's pitch

All you hear is moaning and groaning
Too crowded for roaming
Desperate for the light
See Heaven light up bright

It feels like you are choking
Terror you are invoking
The devil you were promoting
To God you were unknowing

19. Uneven Contradictions

The devil's tricks they often seem
A way to confess through a twisted scheme
When balance falters we're left in despair
Driving us mad when life's unfair

No good exists without its foe
Evil lurks where shadows grow
No happiness shines without some pain
No sun appears without the rain

To believe in God the devil must stay
For light shines bright when dark fades away
Peace is a dream we fight wars to claim
A cycle of chaos always the same

Every crime has a law to defy
Every killer leaves a victim to cry
In love and hate relationships blend
With truth and lies that never end

Air and water life must retain
Filth gives rise to cleanliness gained
Through failure we learn success feels sweet
But every life ends its journey complete

Will Heaven's gates open wide
Or Purgatory be where we reside
Will Hell's fire be our final plea
Only God knows our destiny

20. Vanity

The Devil is mighty bold
Sitting on a pile of gold
Starring at a large mirror
His smile is pure terror

The demons bow low
As he is the King below
Bright gold and jeweled crown
His throne high so he can look down

Dressed in a black suit
An impressive brute
A shirt fire engine red
His appearance will knock you dead

The Devil is clearly cleaver
Knowing he will live forever
To him taking your soul
Never gets old

21. Wrath

His words are full of indignation
Leading others to exasperation
Speaking with condemnation
Handing out retribution

Everyone feels his ferocity
Trying to avoid his hostility
As you are shown his animosity
Against the rules of civility

Society causing his irritation
Showing his frustration
In most situations and communication
Especially with the younger generation

Filled with bitterness
Thoughts are full of vindictiveness
Others happiness he destroys
Their discomfort he enjoys

Talks about his eminence
Looking for vengeance
Handing out judgement
Enjoying the punishment

Doesn't care about the deadly sin
Only about his need to win
Evil is within his skin
Smiling with a wicked grin

www.ingramcontent.com/pod-product-compliance
Lightning Source LLC
LaVergne TN
LVHW050947200726
843508LV00011B/2465